Little Book of Questions & Answers

My Home

Copyright © 1992 Publications International, Ltd. All rights reserved. This book may not be reproduced or quoted in whole or in part by mimeograph or any other printed or electronic means, or for presentation on radio, television, videotape, or film without written permission from:

Louis Weber, C.E.O.
Publications International, Ltd.
7373 North Cicero Avenue
Lincolnwood, Illinois 60646

Permission is never granted for commercial purposes.

Manufactured in U.S.A.

8 7 6 5 4 3 2 1

ISBN: 1-56173-472-1

Contributing Writer: Teri Crawford Jones

Cover Illustration: T. F. Marsh

Book Illustrations: Joe Veno

PUBLICATIONS INTERNATIONAL, LTD.

HARTFORD PUBLIC LIBRARY

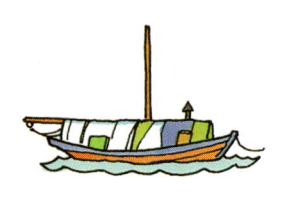

Can you live on a houseboat year-round?
Wherever there's water in the world, you can probably find someone whose year-round home is a houseboat. Some Chinese, Hawaiian, and Japanese people live on houseboats called *sampans.*

What kind of people live in tents?
Goatherders in the desert live in tents that they can pack and move easily to follow their goats from one feeding ground to another. Some people in Scandinavia live in tents and herd reindeer!

How do Eskimos stay warm in an igloo?
The air outside an igloo is cold enough to keep the igloo frozen even though a small fire burns inside. The fire's smoke escapes through a small hole in the igloo's roof.

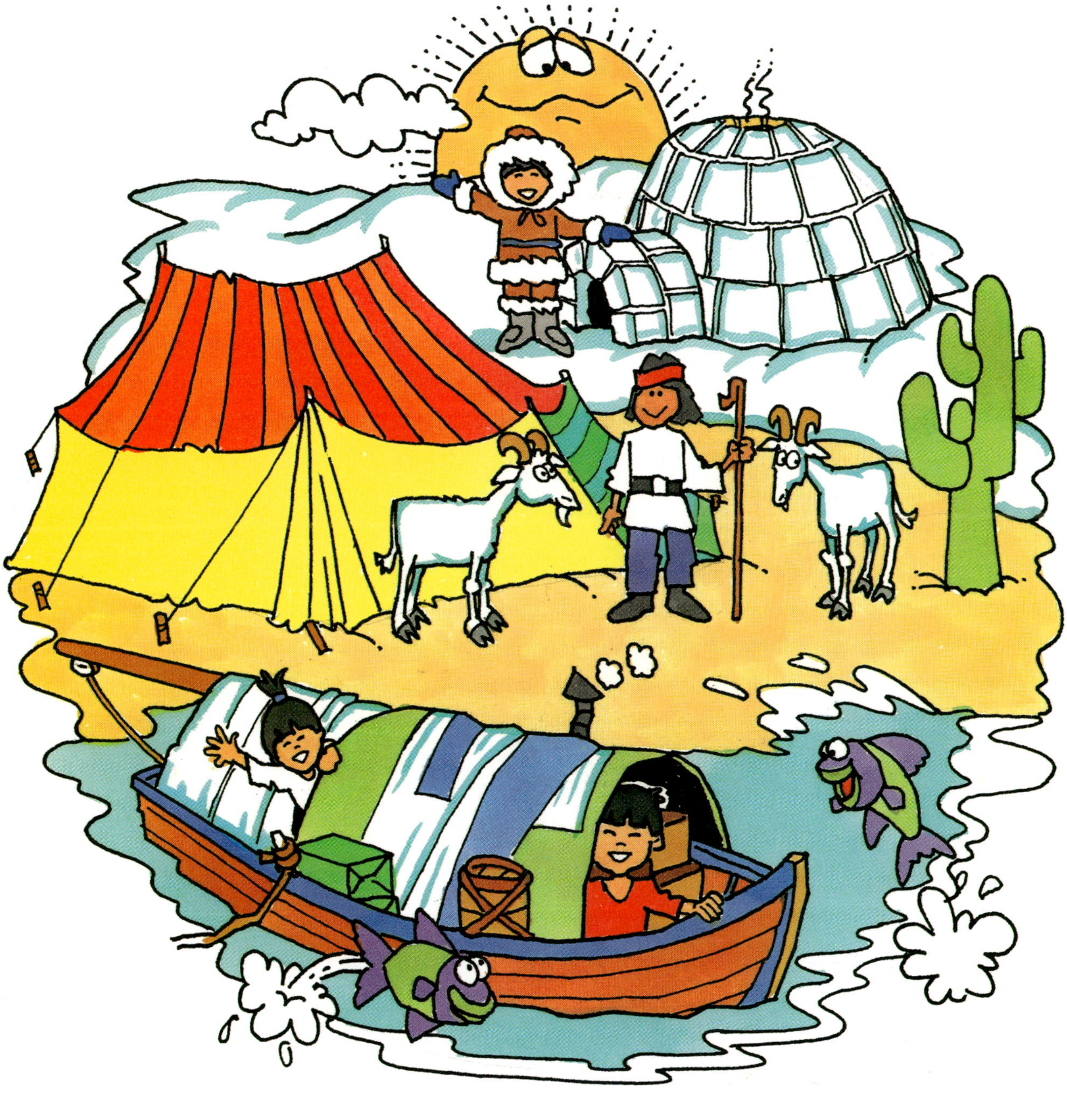

How does a doorbell work?
When you push the doorbell's button, you are sending electricity to a piece of metal called the hammer. The hammer is between two bells. The hammer moves back and forth, hitting the bells.

How does a key unlock a door?
A key is made so that its *teeth* match little parts inside a certain lock. When the key is turned inside the lock, its teeth move those matching parts. The bolt pulls back and the door can be opened.

Why do we have mailboxes?
Mailboxes protect mail from bad weather. They also save lots of time. Mail carriers do not need to wait for an answer to their knock—they drop the mail in the mailbox and go to the next house!

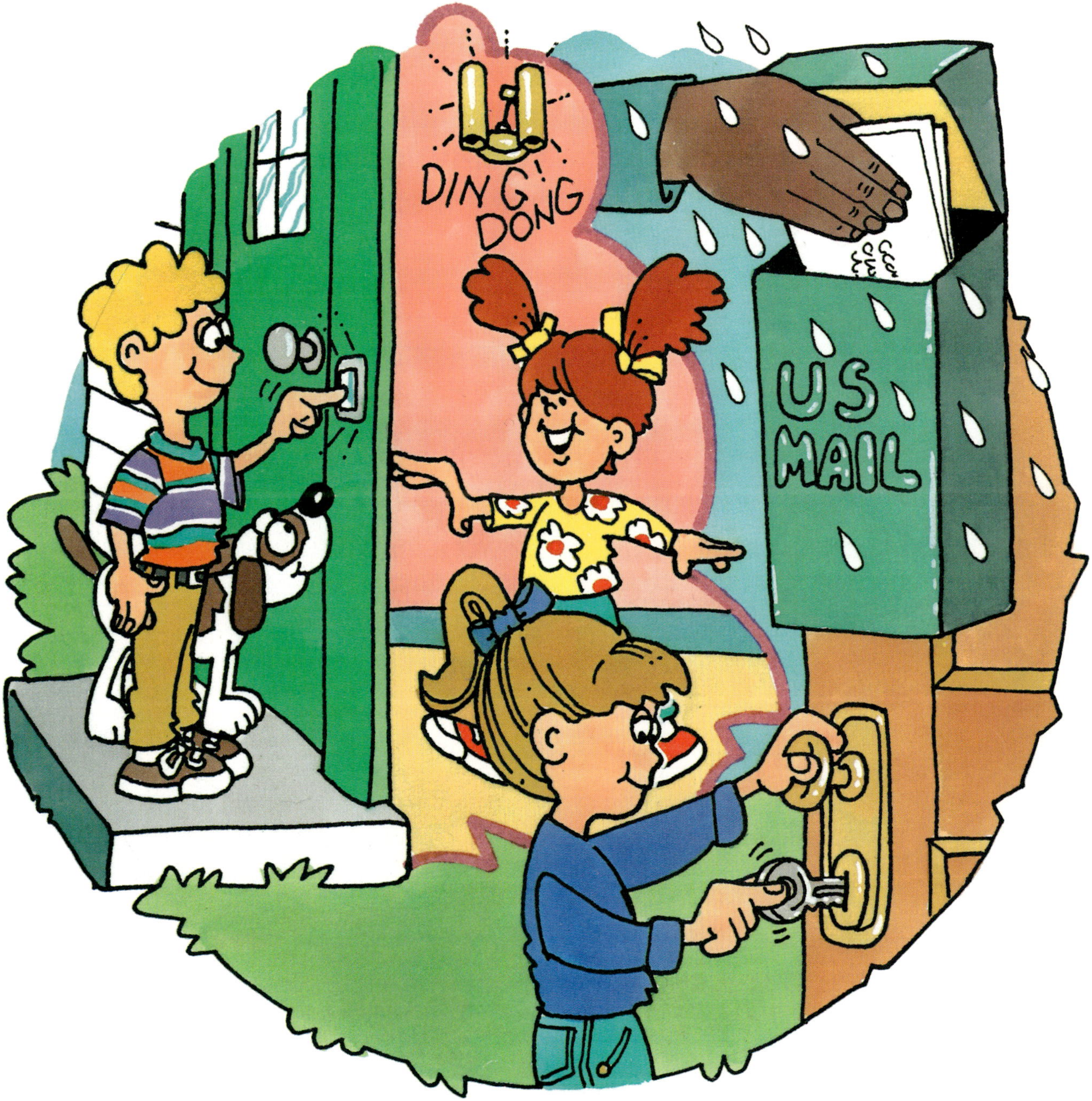
DING DONG
US MAIL

Where do TV shows come from?
TV cameras take pictures. Then the pictures are sent through the air as *signals*. An antenna picks up the signals and sends them into your TV set. The TV set turns the signals back into a picture.

How can we hear voices over the telephone?
When you talk into a phone, your voice is changed into signals that travel through the telephone wires. When your voice signals reach the listener's phone, they change again to sound like your voice.

What makes a light bulb light up?
Electricity makes a thin wire inside the bulb get very hot—so hot that it glows. This special kind of wire glows very brightly for a long time before it burns out.

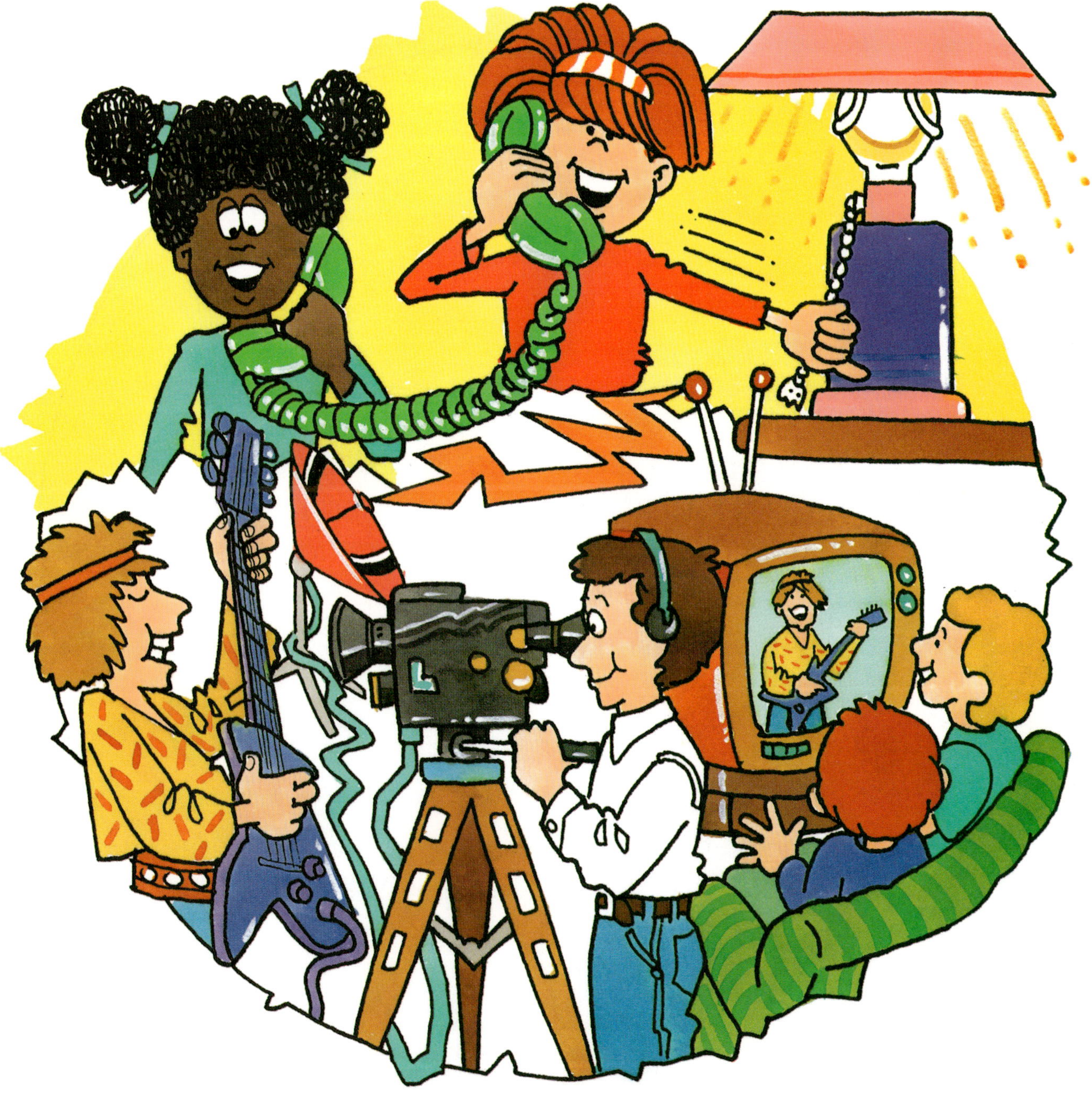

How does a refrigerator stay cold?
In back of a refrigerator are tubes that are filled with very cold liquid. The liquid is pumped through the tubes by a motor. This cold liquid chills the air inside the refrigerator.

How does a dishwasher get dishes clean?
Detergent and very hot water clean the dishes in a dishwasher. Soapy water sprays from the top, bottom, and sometimes sides of the washer to clean all sides of the dirty dishes. The dirty water drains out and clean water rinses the dishes.

How does canned food stay fresh?
Canned food is sealed tight so that no air and no germs can get inside the can. Without air and germs, canned food can stay fresh for a long time!

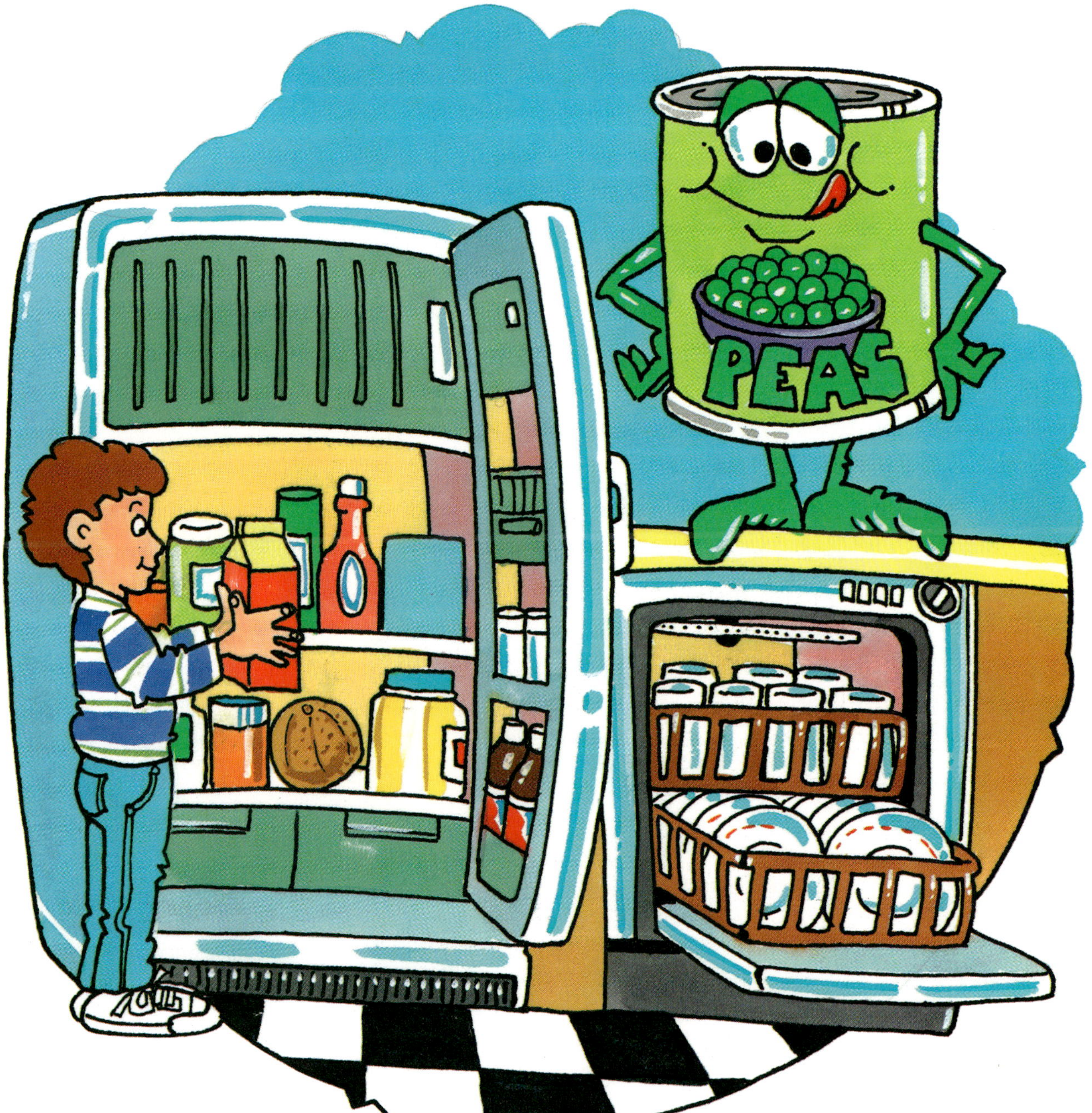
PEAS

Why do ice cubes float?

A cup of liquid water takes up less space than when that cup of water freezes. This means that a cup of frozen water weighs less than a cup of liquid water. The frozen water will float in the liquid water because it is lighter.

Why is there a hole in the bottom of a flowerpot?

Plants need just the right amount of water in their soil—not too little, not too much. The hole in the flowerpot lets extra water drain out of the soil.

Why do people cry when they slice onions?

Onions are juicy. When you cut an onion, tiny droplets of onion juice float in the air and get in your eyes. Tears wash away the stinging onion juice.

HARTFORD PUBLIC LIBRARY

How does an alarm clock work?
Inside a clock are parts that move. When you set the alarm, you are giving these moving parts some instructions. When it reaches your wake-up time, the parts switch on the alarm. Rise and shine!

Why are beds bouncy?
Mattresses have padding and metal springs inside them. The padding makes your mattress soft and comfortable. The springs help support your body when you are sleeping. They make it bouncy, too!

What is inside a pillow?
Some pillows are stuffed with soft feathers. Some are filled with a cottony stuffing called polyester. And some pillows are made of foam rubber. Can you guess what's inside your favorite pillow?

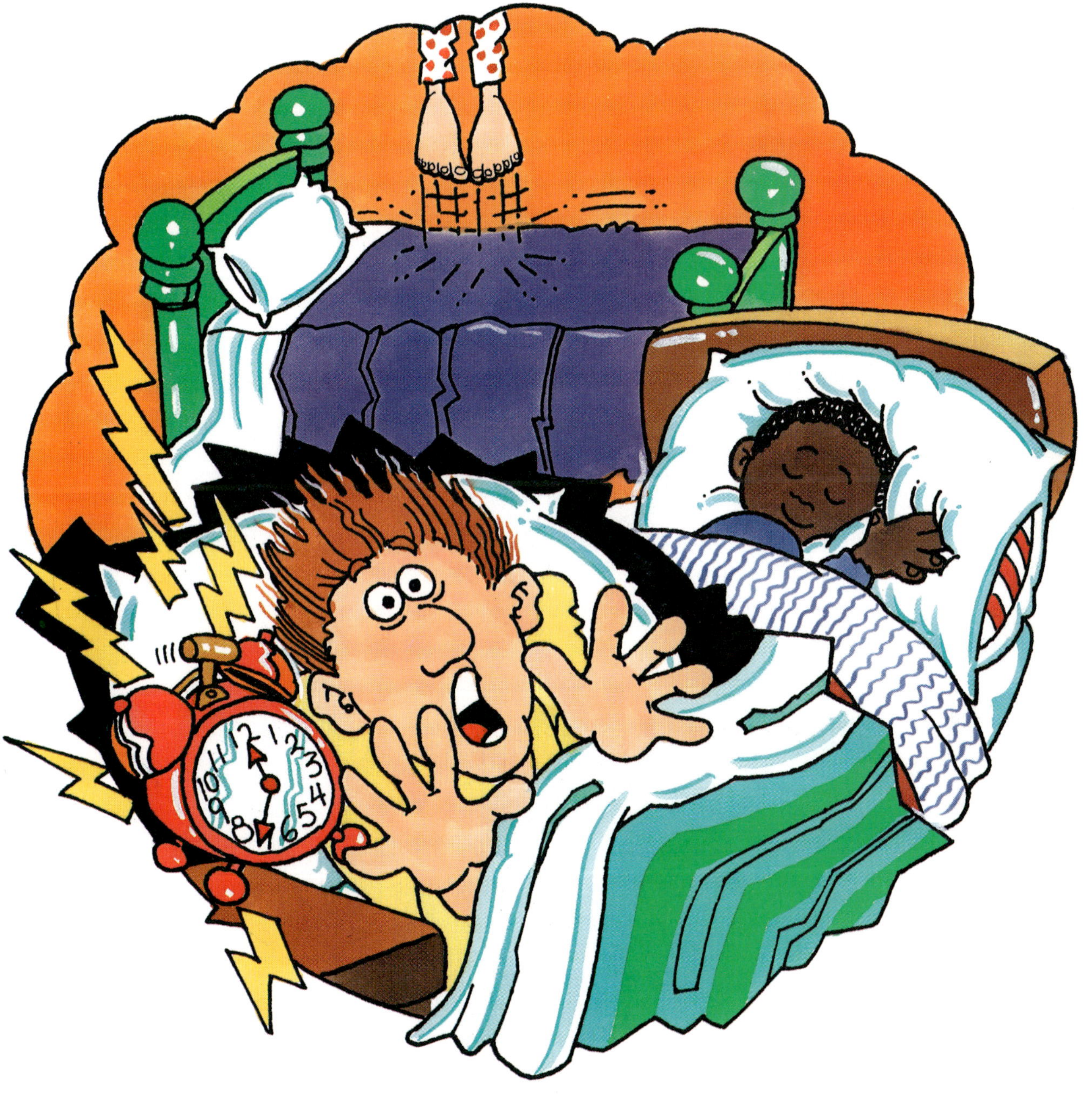

What is inside my teddy bear?
Your teddy bear's stuffing might be soft cotton or it may be foam rubber. And if someone sewed your teddy by hand, it may be stuffed with fabric scraps.

How does a talking toy work?
Inside many talking toys are machines that look like small record players. When you pull the toy's string, a little record spins against a needle and the sound comes out through a speaker.

Why does a ball bounce?
When a rubbery ball is filled with air, it feels hard and tight. When you throw it against something, it "gives" a little and then springs back. That spring makes the ball bounce.

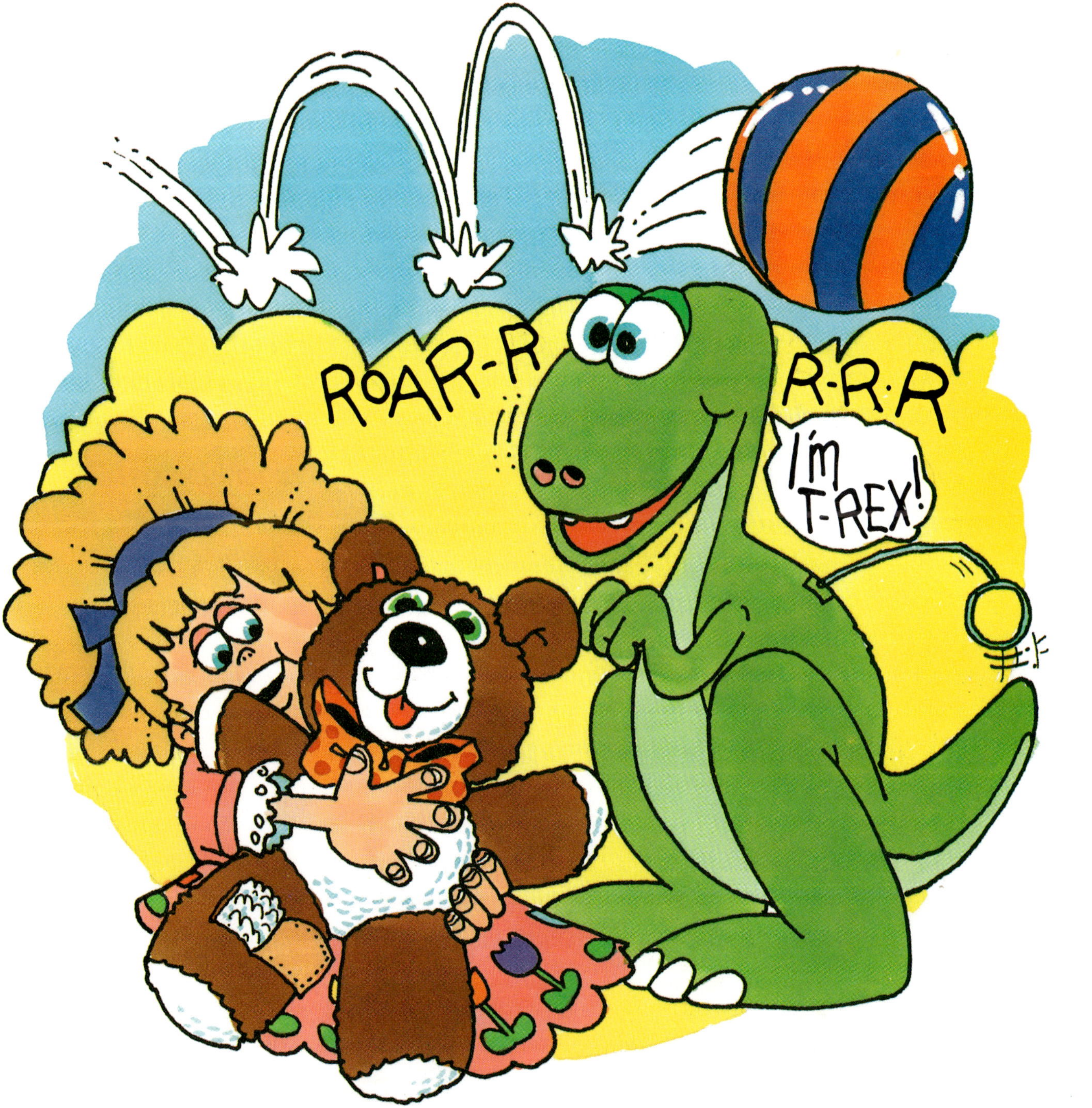
ROAR-R
R-R-R
I'm T-REX!

How are crayons made?
First, wax is melted. Next, colors are added to the wax. The colored wax is then poured into molds. When the colored wax cools, the crayons are unmolded and wrapped with paper.

Why do I shiver when I scratch a chalkboard?
Scratching a chalkboard makes a high, scraping, squeaking noise that hurts our ears and upsets our nerves. It is an awful sound! It often raises goose bumps and makes our hair stand up!

What is clay?
Clay is a kind of soil that has been dug up and cleaned of rocks and twigs until it is very smooth and squishy. Some clay is made by people, though, and comes in pretty colors.

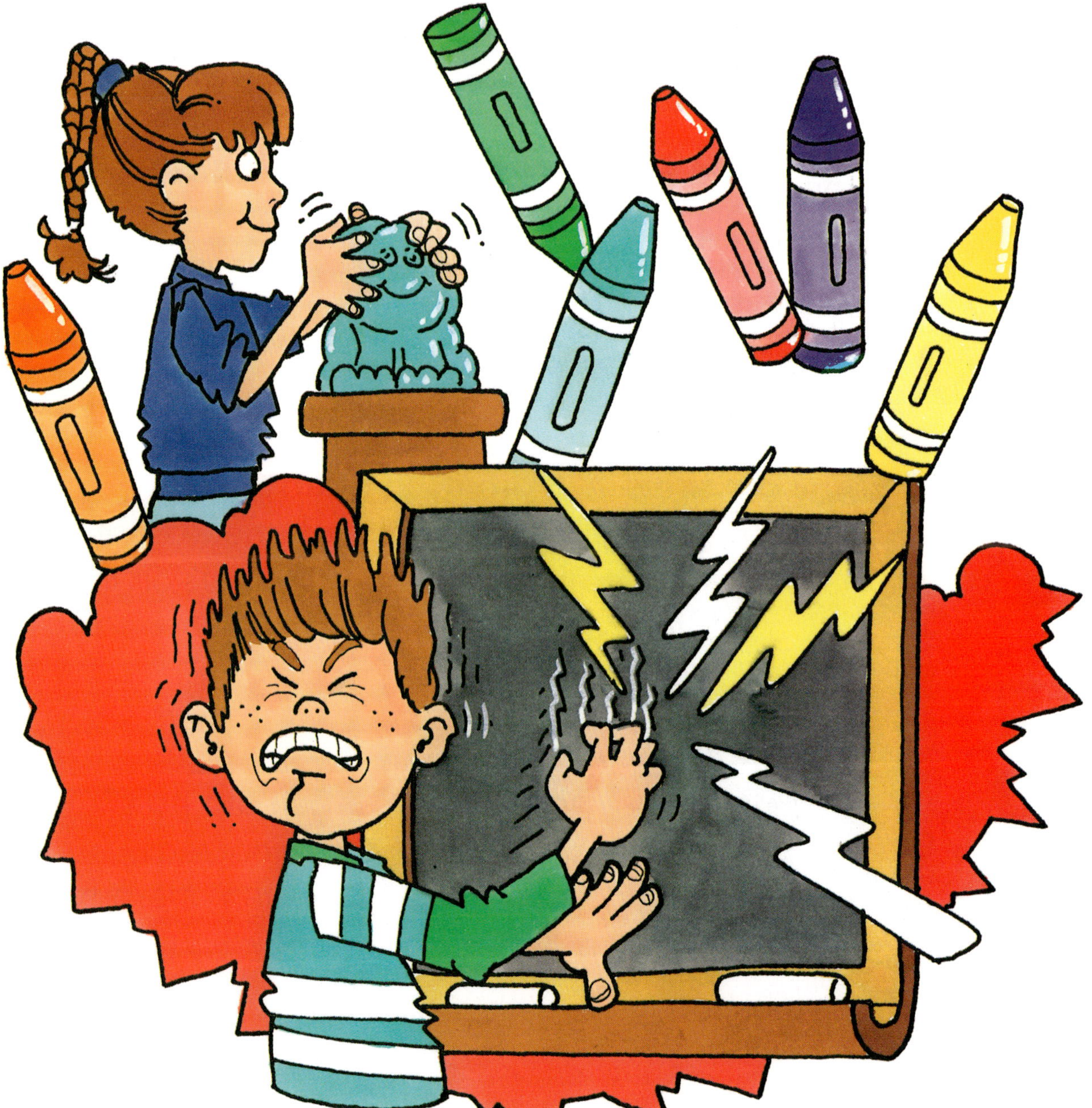

How does water get into the toilet bowl?
Fresh water is stored in the tank at the back of the toilet. When you flush, the water swooshes from the tank into the bowl, and from the bowl down a pipe. More fresh water fills the tank again.

Why are there two drains in a tub?
The drain on the floor of the tub lets the water run out when your bath is over. The drain that's on the wall of the tub helps keep the water from running over if you leave it running by mistake.

Why do we use shampoo to wash our hair?
Hair needs a special cleanser that is not really soap. Soap can leave a sticky film even after it has been rinsed away. Shampoo cleans without leaving a film and it rinses out easily.

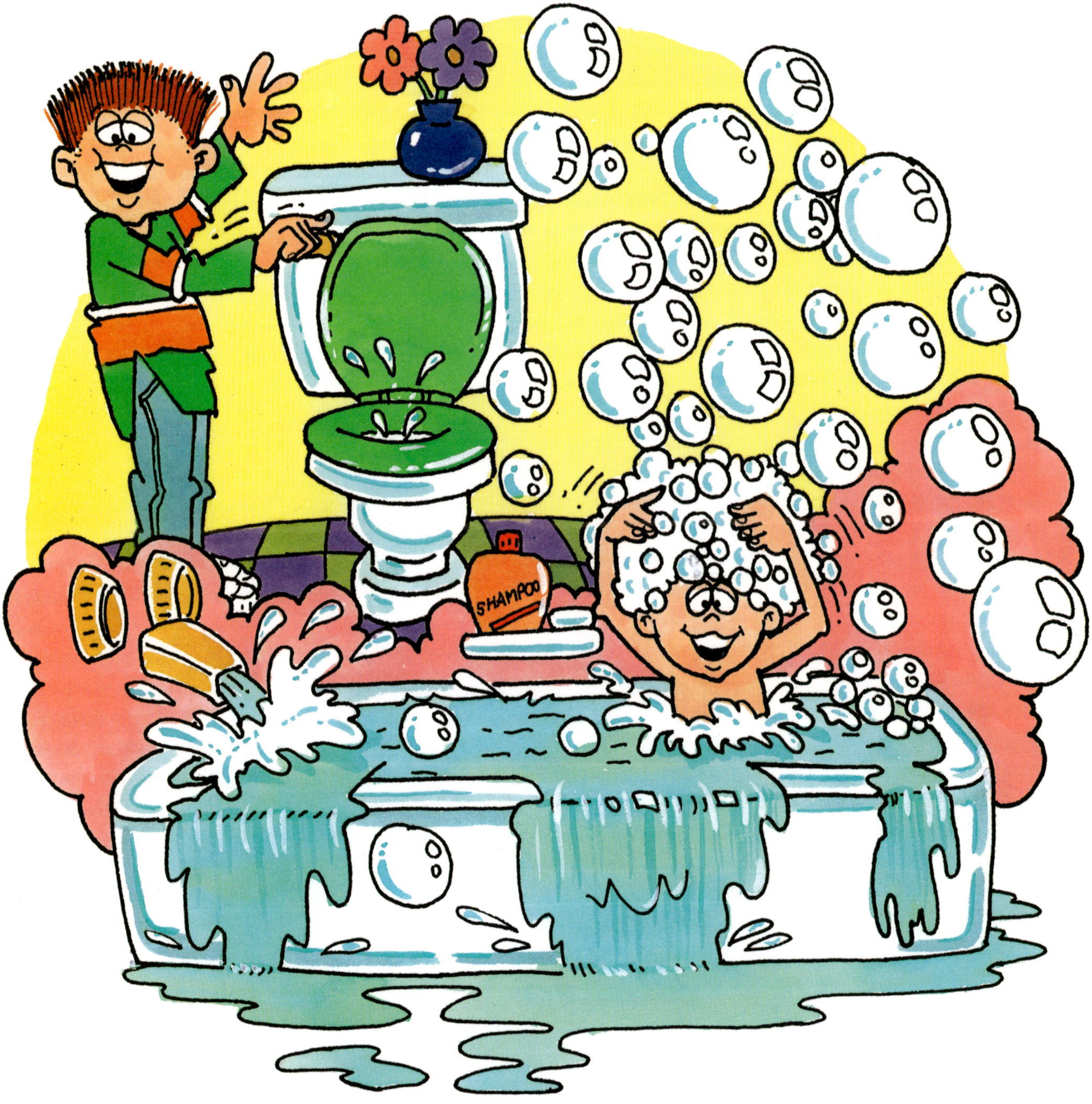
SHAMPOO

Why are basements usually cool?
Outside the basement walls is cool, moist earth. Also, not much sunshine reaches through a basement's windows to warm the air down there.

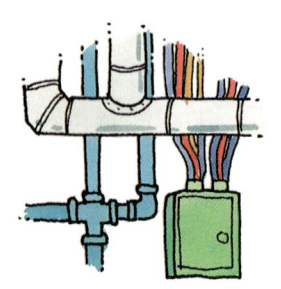

Why are pipes and wires in the basement?
Water runs through a house in pipes. Electricity travels through wires. Heat travels through hot-water pipes or through wider pipes called *ducts*. Upstairs, the pipes and wires are hidden in the walls.

What are fuses and breakers?
Too many electrical things turned on at once can be dangerous. Fuses and breakers can stop the flow of electricity before it becomes dangerous. "Blowing a fuse" or "throwing a breaker" gives us a chance to turn off some electricity.

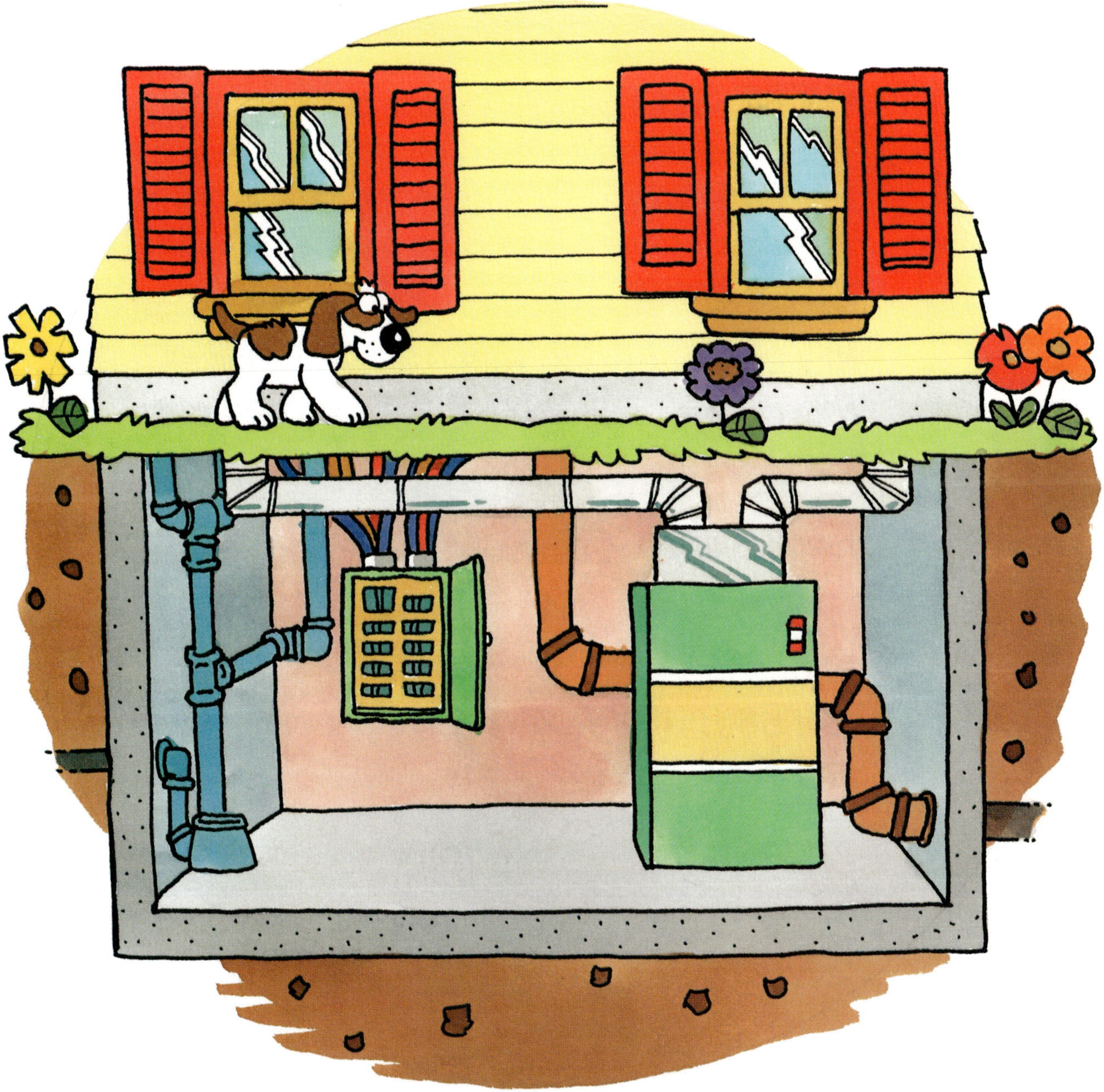

Why do socks cling to other clothes?

As clothes tumble in the dryer, they rub together and make *static electricity*. Socks often make lots of static electricity. And static electricity makes clothes—especially socks—cling together.

Why do we separate our laundry by colors?

Many clothing colors "run." If you were to wash a white shirt with red towels, the shirt would probably turn pink. It is a good idea to wash clothes with similarly colored things.

How does an iron get wrinkles out?

Heat makes wrinkles go away—and irons are very hot! The flat bottom of an iron smooths out the fabric even more. Some irons use moist steam to smooth wrinkles.

HARTFORD PUBLIC LIBRARY

Why does dust make me sneeze?
Pieces of dust are so small that they float in the air and get in your nose. It tickles—*ACHOO!* A sneeze helps your nose get rid of dust and other tickly things.

Why is a vacuum cleaner noisy?
A vacuum cleaner has a loud, powerful motor that sucks up dirt and stores it in a special bag. It also has brushes that sweep up crumbs and other bits of things. All this makes a lot of noise!

What is a sponge made of?
A real sponge was once a living sea animal! But most sponges that we use around the house were made in a factory. They are usually made of foam rubber.

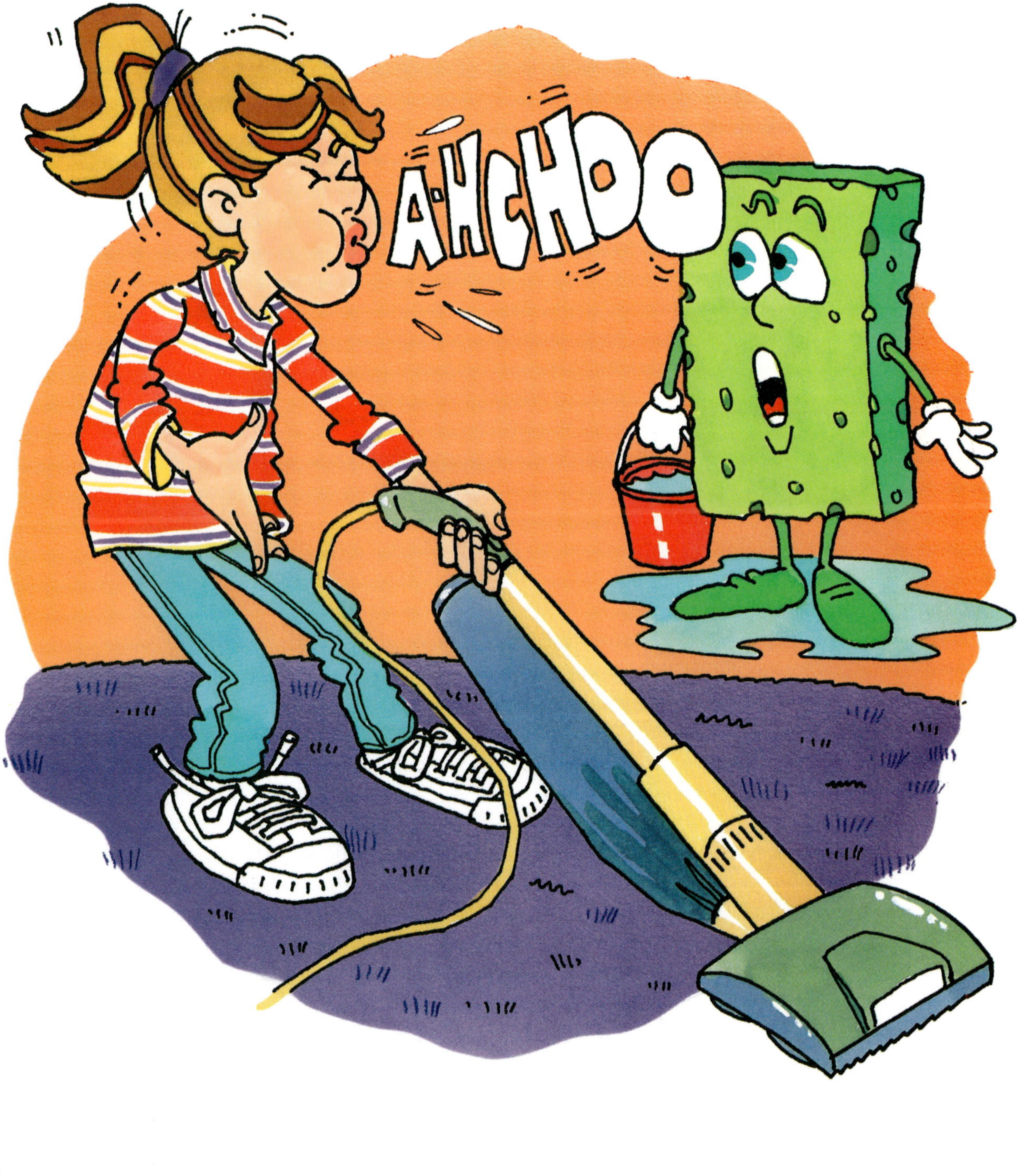
A-HCHOO

How does "pumping" help me swing?
Pumping a swing is like giving yourself a push. Leaning forward pushes the swing back; leaning back pushes the swing forward. The harder you pump, the higher you'll swing!

Why can't I teeter-totter by myself?
Teeter-totters only work if two people take turns pushing off the ground. If you sit on one end without someone on the other, you won't go anywhere. Teeter-totters work best if both riders weigh about the same.

Why does a kite need a tail?
A kite's tail keeps the kite steady so it does not spin in circles and get tangled. Some kites are made so they do not need tails.

HARTFORD PUBLIC LIBRARY

Why does popcorn pop?
Inside a kernel of popcorn is water and something called *starch*. When the kernel gets very hot, the water turns to steam and the starch swells up. Suddenly the hard shell of the kernel breaks open and the white starch pops out!